PRAISE FOR *Lead Your Whole Life* :

"We all need a coach to help us navigate to growth. Jessica is a coach with a track record of helping people press in to their growth process. She has distilled her wisdom here. Let her walk with you on your journey. Her holistic perspective will show you not only where you may need to grow, but how to get there. Dive into it and watch your life begin to change!"

Seth Barnes | FOUNDER OF ADVENTURES IN MISSIONS

"This will wake your spirit up! Diving into the "leader" we all have inside and start to explore, revive, and take hold of our life we are meant to live out. A diamond in the rough! In a fast-paced, high-stressed to perform and a constant comparison environment that creates expectations we can't control, Jessica shows us what we can control and how important it is to look within and free ourselves to live out the life we are meant to live. Healthy, Whole, and Purpose driven!"

Angela Toler | MENTOR, LIFE COACH AND FUNCTIONAL NUTRITIONIST

Lead Your Whole Life

How Cultivating Wholeness
Transforms the Way We Live and Lead

Jessica Dahl

Published by:

Your Whole Purpose

Kirkland, Washington

www.YourWholePurpose.com

Editor: Carol Killman Rosenberg

Book Design: Sara Wondergem

Cover and Logo Design: Megan Melseth

Acknowledgements

First and foremost, I have to express my gratitude to those who have been an influential piece in my life. The people I cherish the most is my family. My parents and siblings have walked each season of life with me and have supported every single season and endeavor. If it weren't for your belief and support, I wouldn't be the woman I am today; words can't describe how grateful I am for each of you. This book has years of knowledge that I have learned from many others, and I am so grateful for the opportunity to have learned from some of the greatest leaders and mentors in my life. For all my good friends and mentors who have cheered me up when I needed it, pushed me further than I ever thought my limits could go, and challenged me to believe in myself, I am forever thankful. For anyone who has been a part of my life, you know who you are; you have impacted me in one way or another, thank you. This is just the beginning!

Contents

Lead Your Whole Life

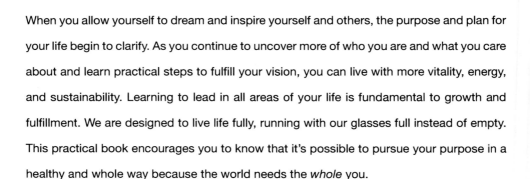

When you allow yourself to dream and inspire yourself and others, the purpose and plan for your life begin to clarify. As you continue to uncover more of who you are and what you care about and learn practical steps to fulfill your vision, you can live with more vitality, energy, and sustainability. Learning to lead in all areas of your life is fundamental to growth and fulfillment. We are designed to live life fully, running with our glasses full instead of empty. This practical book encourages you to know that it's possible to pursue your purpose in a healthy and whole way because the world needs the *whole* you.

This book started off as a blog I was writing for myself. I took information I had written years ago, added my thoughts about things I've learned and cared about, and then kept researching. I then realized this was beneficial material for my friends, clients, and anyone for that matter, so I decided to make a book out of it! I know that many of us can have good intentions for our lives; yet without action, good intentions don't take us anywhere. Taking action steps can be daunting, so I wanted to make sure this book was practical for everyone in any area of life. You can come back to this in any season to refocus and gain clarity and direction.

Personally, I know what it's like to be unaware of all these topics that we will discuss, and now I am grateful to have cultivated wholeness in my own life and I desire to share the importance of this with others. I am excited to see where this leads you. My desire is that this book would inspire you, equip you, and then empower you to uncover more of your whole purpose, how to do it in a healthy and whole way, and then learn how you can lead others well. This is bringing the concept of "wholeness" to another level!

What Does It Mean to Lead Your Whole Life?

In our communities and world in general, there is a missing link between being a high achiever and living life with vitality. Despite their success, leaders and high achievers seem to be experiencing a lot of burnout and imbalances in many areas of their lives. I believe when more people know their own "why," understand their worth and value, and live their purposes, while taking care of themselves as a whole, they will be able to lead each area of their lives with fulfillment, joy, and sustainability.

The truth is, there are many people who have lost hope due to hard circumstances, life transitions, and more. When hope or lack of direction is lost, it leads to a loss of purpose or drive. It's easy to place focus on one area of life, such as our career or our family, so much that when it shifts or unexpected changes arise, we have no idea what to do with ourselves. There are many areas that make up your life, and as you learn to unpack what they are from this book, you will begin to see that you *are* the leader of your life.

You may be thinking, *But I am not a leader.* Well, guess what . . . yes, you are. You are the leader of your own life, and you are a leader to those around you. You get to choose how you lead it and them. You are the creator of the life you are living, so it's time to embark on a journey to lead yourself well in all areas of your life.

First and foremost, you can't give anything from any empty cup. If your life is constantly running dry, or you are always tired, or you feel like you're on overload, then you have nothing to give others. In other words, you can't pour water from an empty cup. Just like your life, in order to give anything to others, you first need to lead your whole life well and keep your personal cup full. Only then you can live your purpose more fully and pour your overflowing cup more powerfully into others' cups.

The word "whole" in *Merriam-Webster's* dictionary is defined as "free of defect or impairment, physically sound and healthy: free of disease or deformity, mentally or emotionally sound." Although you may go through life experiencing many changes, growth, and seasons, you have the ability to see yourself as a whole, complete, new person with each transformation.

You are the only one who has the authority over your life. Not even your spouse, children, friends, workplace, place of worship, etc., have control over your life. It's you who's responsible for choosing how you live and how you feel. It's no one else's responsibility but your own. You are on this earth with the ability to thrive in your life with reasons to jump out of bed in the morning greeting the new day with enthusiasm.

Activation

To begin, try this exercise: Think of how you are currently living your life. If you managed each aspect of your life for the next five years just the same as you do now, do you think you would feel great? Would you feel burnt out? Would you love your life? Let your answer sink in and get real with yourself.

Now, sit in a comfortable position where all distractions are minimized, and take about three minutes to close your eyes and imagine how you want to feel in the life you desire. What do you hope to feel as you step into your future? You may find it hard to sit still for a moment and remain focused on this feeling. Each time your mind begins to drift away to other thoughts, come back to the feelings you want to feel. Is it happiness, freedom, light, love, peace, joy, patience? All these emotions are wonderful. Stay in the feeling for another minute.

When you open your eyes, be sure to write down what the life you desire feels like so you can always return to it for a reminder. You will now step into learning so much more about yourself and how you can lead your whole life toward those desires. When you know what you want to feel, this awareness can direct you to the steps to get there. You do not want to be overwhelmed by all the ways you want to change or improve your life, so choose one step in the "action steps" in each category in this book to get closer to your desired whole life. When you accomplish the first step, keep adding more steps as you move toward your heart's desires. That's what this book is all about: activating your desires to become reality.

A way to make sure you get the most out of this book is to share and discuss these topics with your friends or choose someone you can be accountable to. You may find some strategies that work for you and others that don't work for you. That is totally fine! Take this info, try it out, leave what you don't want, and pursue what you do want.

What Does Your Whole-Self Mean?

As humans, we are intricate machines, and we need to understand the way our intricacies work to understand the importance of why it matters that we care for ourselves.

I will never forget a powerful time during my life-changing experience in Thailand. I felt like I needed to do a challenge, a month and a half of studying six different topics, a different one each week, and it included eating healthy food and getting exercise. The topics covered different systems: physical, mental, emotional, and spiritual. I learned the important role each of these play in our everyday lives and how they make up the whole person we are. We are not complete without understanding how all these systems work together. In this book, you will go through many areas of your life and learn the importance of all aspects of life functioning properly together-that is, synergistically.

We are constantly at battle trying to find balance and wholeness in all areas of our lives. When these areas work toward alignment, we are able to give more from a cup that is full rather than one that is running low or nearly empty. Keep in mind, we will likely never reach a place in our lives where everything is fully balanced, yet the goal is to move toward balance. The way we function best is when we serve others from our overflow.

We also do not want to ignore the fact that our finances, community, career contribution, and fun are all part of our lives, and if we focus on one more than another, we'll feel the pull of imbalances all over our lives.

Chapter-by-Chapter Action Step

In each chapter to follow, I'll discuss key points, which offer you tangible tools to learn how to create more self-awareness and cultivate wholeness which will allow you to lead others in a healthy way. In each "action step," you will have an opportunity to rate yourself on a scale of 1–10; 1 is your lowest point and 10 is your highest point. Then you will choose one action step to get one step closer to a 10. We will rarely be at a 10 in all areas of our lives, yet the key is to move toward that level while growing every day.

Identity

First and foremost, knowing your identity is more powerful than what you feel or think of yourself. No matter your faith background, you are not here on this earth by accident. You are here with a bigger intention and purpose than you may realize. You impact this world by being who you are. You were created in God's image, the creator of the universe, and that's a pretty big deal!

There's a reason you have specific skills, talents, and abilities. You are wired to live a life fully yourself and no one else. You are worthy. You are beautiful. You are loved. You are cherished. You are special. You are generous. You are talented. You are strong. You are confident. You are genuine. You are funny. You are joyful. You are (insert whatever you feel).

When you are living "fully you," life flows through you. You don't have to try, force, or manipulate anything or anyone. Speaker, author, and pastor, Andy Stanley says, "Where life flows, influence grows."[1] We all have influence with at least one person in our lives. The only way to really influence is if we are being our honest self and letting life flow through us. Getting to know yourself so you can be yourself and then give of yourself is the most valuable gift you can give others. We never want to live a stagnant life where we only live for ourselves. As you are uniquely, fully you, which is a gift to others, remember to have others around you who believe in you, encourage you, and challenge you to become the best version of yourself you can be. Who are some people you trust in your life who can mentor, encourage, or coach you?

Worth and Value

How often do you find yourself believing you are worth less than someone else? I think about how social media seems to be taking over most of our lives these days. We spend hours scrolling through what seems to be people's seemingly perfect lives while our own lives seem messy. Then comparison creeps in, and we tend to lose sight of who we really are and focus on what we think we need to be "more of" or "less of." Sometimes we focus on these comparisons or on the things we've done or what has been done to us, and we let them define our value and worth. If we hear something enough times, we generally begin to believe it is true.

Self-love, self-respect, self-worth—there is a reason why all these words start with "self." You cannot find them in anyone else. There's nothing you can do and nothing that can be done to you to change your worth no matter how broken, bruised, or beat up you may be.

Vulnerability

One aspect that we don't always pay attention to is the power of sharing our stories. If you think about it, we as humans connect in a powerful way when we are vulnerable and share from our brokenness and the real-life struggles we go through. Of course, this doesn't mean you need to go shouting about all your problems from the rooftop, but it's healthy to surround yourself with people you trust so you can share what's going on in your real life. This reminds you and others that it is OK to not be OK, it is OK to struggle. It is OK to not know it all—you are human! This is one place I used to struggle with, and it's still hard sharing my struggles because I want to seem like I am strong. Remember this: the one who can be the most vulnerable is usually the strongest one.

Here are three reminders to why sharing your story is so vital:

You are not alone:

Sometimes in life the situations you go through are rough. You may feel like you are the only one who has ever felt this way or there is no way out. Oftentimes when you share your story, you find you are not the only one who has felt that way. And God often reveals to you through the Holy Spirit (or your inner knowing, your gut) and community how you can begin to move forward. How refreshing!

Shame:

With most of our struggles and insecurities, we tend to hold a sense of guilt or shame whether we realize it or not. There is power in sharing our stories because we dismantle the power of shame. What you keep in the dark becomes a foothold where lies seem true. When you bring things into the light, this power over you is lost. This is good news. There is hope!

Freedom:

There is no freedom in what is kept in the darkness. The more you keep to yourself, the more suppressed you feel. There is liberation in speaking up because now there is no hiding, and everything is brought to light. There is space for freedom for yourself and for others with whom you share.[2]

Self-Awareness

To build healthy relationships with yourself, family, and friends, to do well in your career, and to lead others, you need to have a high level of self-awareness. To have self-awareness and emotional intelligence, you need to constantly learn everything you can about yourself and love every area of yourself, even as you grow. As you cultivate self-awareness, you will discover your skills, talents, abilities, passions, and fears, you will learn from your past, and you will have clarity on what you desire for your future. This will enable you to understand whether you are engaging in healthy relationships and workplaces, and if you are ultimately living into the purpose that is designed specifically for you. Being aware in all areas of your life is key to moving forward in a healthy way in your body, mind, emotions, relationships, finances, career, and passions.

Let's talk about the body for a minute. Have you ever gotten sick and it took a toll on your whole day, week, or month? Sickness is what happens when something in your body is out of alignment; this is when you don't function at your prime. If your health fails, every area of your life is affected. The way you treat your family, your coworkers, and yourself when you don't feel like yourself ends up costing more than just your health. Minor body aches and pains, fatigue, indigestion, and major health issues that can paralyze and affect the fulfillment of your life. A huge step in the right direction is self-awareness. The more you understand your body, the clearer you are in how to best take care of yourself.

In Change Your Posture, Change Your Life, author Richard Brennan says, "A certain action that is produced over and over again, which, if it goes unchecked, turns into habitual behavior. This habitual reaction will eventually feel normal and natural to us."[3]

If what Brennan says is true, you have the power to produce healthy actions in all areas of your life that can eventually lead to a full life you love. It is possible. You choose the life you desire.

Fear

I have heard many people say fear is **F**alse **E**vidence **A**ppearing **R**eal. Fear is something we all deal with in our lives because we are human. Fear is basically our perception of our current reality and what it means to us. The emotions we feel when we're afraid, such as anxiety, confusion, anger, etc., are very real feelings. Yet the fear itself is made up by us.

To stop letting your fear keep you from making choices to move in the direction you desire, you have to realize that your fear is a false reality. For example, I grew up singing, dancing, and creating performances at home for my friends and family. I don't have a fear of public speaking. In fact, I actually love it! But I do have a fear of speaking in front of a camera. For whatever reason, I freeze up and forget what I was going to talk about in the first place. Especially if there is a videographer on the other end. I feel like I either look too stiff, that I won't get all the words out that I want to say, or that I will say a thousand uhm's. I recognize that my nervous, anxious feelings are real, but the fear is my own perception. The only way for me to work on this is to keep practicing and keep showing up to speak on videos.

I read an article where Carl Jung quoted, "If there is a fear of falling, the only safety is deliberately jumping."[4] Merriam-Webster's Dictionary defines the word "deliberately" as "with full awareness of what one is doing." This means to do something on purpose, with intention! That means whatever you fear is not going to feel safe, but you get to choose how you're going to go through it. Again, fears are not real. They are created by a series of events that happened to you or that you have seen happen to others in the past. Fear becomes a wall not to cross to keep things familiar so that whatever you're afraid of doesn't happen to you. When you run from fear, that is when you allow it to control you.

We all have fears. They will always come up. The question is not about how to get rid of fear but instead how to go confidently through that which you fear even if you're scared.

To work on going through the fear, you have to allow yourself to feel the uncomfortable emotions and sit with them until they are real to you, then you can let go of the fear. When you let go of something, you are not giving up; rather, you release of control of the fear and trust that you can go through the situation anyway. When you begin to feel anxious or fearful, ask yourself, "What am I attached to here?" Generally, you are attached to some sort of outcome. Once you notice what that attachment is, you will be able to begin releasing that fear.

Lead Fear Action Step

Here's a challenge for you: List your most troublesome fears. After you list them honestly, write yourself a letter about what your fear is constantly telling you. For example: "I am not good enough," or "I will never be like my mom [or whomever]," or "I don't have the skills to make it happen," or "I will never be loved." After you write this letter, write a second letter to yourself talking to your fear and telling your fear that it's not welcome anymore. Then write about what it would be like to have freedom and own the opposite side of your fear.

Lead Fear Action Step Planning

_____
_____
_____
_____
_____
_____
_____
_____
_____
_____
_____
_____
_____
_____
_____
_____
_____
_____
_____
_____
_____
_____
_____
_____
_____
_____
_____
_____

Lead Your Body

Movement

Our bodies are extremely intricate, and we need to pay attention to how they work in order to take care of them. What if you fall and can't get back up? That question may be a bit dramatic because many people, no matter their health, can get back up when they physically fall. However, our bodies are designed in such a specific way that if we don't take care of them, our strength diminishes, our energy slows down, our joints hurt, and long term-chronic effects can begin to take place.

The key to a more vibrant, healthy, and sustained life is to move your body. It's not about exercise; it's about getting the blood flowing through your body to your brain and about being strong for the things you accomplish in a day and maybe for your children. It's about the energy you will have for your passions and purposes. Do anything you enjoy that gets your body moving, and you will appreciate how your body is able to do so.

Your body is like a machine that is constantly giving you feedback through symptoms that are speaking to your mind and trying to tell you something is either right or wrong. Every time you feel an ache, pain, or notice that something feels "off," that is your body's flashing light saying there is something that needs attention.

We have a physical body that was created to move. According to acefitness.org, here are some interesting facts about the body: The human body takes about twelve hours to digest food; there are about 37.2 trillion cells in an adult human body; the human heart beats about 100,000 times a day; adults blink on average of 10 times per minute; and the human body contain about 5.5 liters of blood.[5] So, clearly, the inside of your body (your organs, cells, blood, etc.) is constantly moving. Now imagine if you just sat around all day long: everything on the inside would begin to slow down.

Here are some benefits to moving your body: lower resting heart rate, better control of body fat, immune function strengthened, muscular strength increased, better stabilization of blood sugar, improved function of the cardiovascular system, better joint health, higher quality of sleep, and improved digestion. I'm not going to suggest the best way to work out for you. It is up to you to discover what you enjoy and what works best for your body.

I love to go outdoors on hikes, runs, snowboarding, surfing, or bike riding. I also love kickboxing, dancing, my personal yoga and workouts I create alone, and workout classes with others. Mixing it up keeps it really fun, and I know my body and mind well enough for what I need. What you need doesn't need to be extreme; try out different activities and see what your body needs. What do you need to make activity part of your lifestyle, something you will stick with instead of something you will eventually drop?

Lead Movement Action Step

First, rate yourself on a scale of 1–10 where you are at with your movement lifestyle. Second, choose one step you can take to get closer to a level 10. How can you add body movement that you actually enjoy into your lifestyle?

Lead Movement Action Step Journaling

Food is Fuel

To achieve a healthier, more balanced lifestyle, you must change your eating habits and eat smart. Remember, it's not about getting full; it's about eating a balanced diet and getting proper nutrition. If we treat our bodies as they were created to be treated and eat balanced, fresh, and healthy foods, our bodies will respond with greater health. We will feel better, feel stronger, have more energy, and live longer. Food is fuel to feel your most energetic and to keep going.

Are you tired of all the fad diets that are out there? It seems to me that they go in phases. One will be in style for a while, then another joins the cause. Honestly, it can be confusing and frustrating; I have been there. I am not a certified nutritionist, yet through my experiences as a certified wellness and life coach, yoga instructor, and fitness instructor, I have learned that every person's body is different and what may be healthy for me wouldn't be healthy for you. If you have never seen a nutritionist or a naturopath, or if you haven't had blood tests to learn what foods are best for your body, I highly recommend doing so to begin fueling your body with what you need. You could be eating "healthy" food, but for you those foods could be toxins.

If you are constantly traveling or doing service work in other countries, I have a few ideas for you. Years back, I traveled with a missions organization, Adventures in Missions, on The World Race for a year. We took a backpack and tent and lived in a different country each month to do service projects, build orphanages, teach English, work in churches, work with eradicating slavery and human trafficking organizations, and more. Because of my background in the wellness industry, I found a need that hadn't been met yet: people on the mission field or those who were constantly traveling didn't know how they could still be healthy without the routines they had at home.

I'm here to say that finding a consistent healthy eating routine as well as exercise is not only something that is healthy for us to do, but it is also necessary. You will have to do some research about the country or city you will be visiting or living in to learn what foods are available to you and then choose the healthy options. I have seen many benefits in myself and others who have chosen to do so. If you are going to be traveling or doing mission work serving others, it's necessary to take good care of yourself; otherwise, you can't serve anyone else well.

Mindful Eating

Do you find yourself eating just because you know you need food in you? Or do you eat really good food so fast you realized you didn't even enjoy it? I find myself doing both. The reality is, you won't really know what types of food are best for your body unless you begin to notice the way your body responds to them. Food is fuel for our bodies; it gives us life. When you take time to enjoy the tastes, textures, and sensations, you notice endorphins ("feel-good" hormones) rush through your body when you eat. It's important to be mindful of what you are putting in your body and how it is affecting you, whether positively or negatively. It is healthy to be mindful of all you put into your mouth.

While being mindful of what you are eating, you also want to know "why" you are eating. Before you take a bite of food, ask yourself: Am I eating because I am actually hungry? Am I eating because I am stressed? Am I eating as an escape to procrastinate from what I need to be focusing on? Is my food comfort when other things fail me? Do I have hormonal imbalances that cause me to want to eat certain foods? The first step is self-awareness; the second is being honest with yourself and admitting what the core purpose of your eating is.

As you begin to know yourself more, you will notice the difference when you have healthy eating habits and when you're allowing your unhealthy habits to rule your life. There is always an underlying factor to "why" you do everything you do, even with eating food.

Toxins

Being a wellness and life coach has gotten me to listen to my body to get to the root issues of my own health goals. I had symptoms of fatigue, brain fog, and achy muscles for a period of time, and it was affecting my personal and professional life. I felt exhausted and needed some answers. I began keeping a health journal, one that I give to clients to use, and I noticed when my body responded negatively and positively to food, exercise, and daily routines. After seeing my naturopath and neurolink practitioner, I learned that my body was extremely toxic, stemming from emotional distress I didn't even realize was there.

Neurolink is basically rewiring and resetting the body and brain to connect to each other. Since our physical, mental, emotional, and spiritual parts of us are all connected, it's important that we are aware if anything is off balance or not functioning at its full potential. This is just one practice I have chosen to add into my personal wellness journey. I recommend not taking my experience as your own but to find what works best for you. Through my wellness journey, I have learned about toxic buildup and that you can be a health-minded person, but if you aren't doing the right things to meet your body's needs, what you think is healthy could actually be toxic to your body. When that happens, your body begins to fight itself, causing symptoms such as fatigue, joint pain, brain fog, and more. Toxins can enter the body in so many forms, internally by the food we eat, mentally by the thoughts we think, emotionally by internal stress, and environmentally by the chemicals that surround us. Unless you live in a bubble, you have toxins all around and there is no way to eliminate fully, yet there are some you can control.

Begin looking at the foods you eat, the products you purchase, and what you are exposed to. Use this information to keep yourself as free from toxins as possible. It doesn't seem like toxins have an enormous effect on your life until, like stress, you are constantly surrounded by them and they slowly begin to cause damage in other parts of your body, such as your gut, liver, gallbladder, brain, and more. It's better to be forward-thinking by knowing you can prevent long-term damage than to have to repair the damage later. Take a look at Michelle Brown's book Energy Reset for more information on toxins.

Lead Nutrition Action Step

First, rate yourself on a scale of 1–10 where you are at with your nutritional lifestyle. Second, to get closer to a level 10, what is one step you can take to add healthy, balanced nutrition into your lifestyle?

Take time to sit in a quiet place without your phone, TV, or any other distractions and slowly eat your food. Notice what a difference it makes in the experience of what food does for your body, mind, and soul. If you feel like you are still discovering what foods work and don't work for your body, keep a food journal. Try doing this for a week, and then try to keep the journal for a month to see how you feel after every meal or snack you eat or drink. At the end of each day, log the time of day you ate, include any meals, snacks, or drinks you consumed, and write down whether your body responded well or worse after each meal or beverage. There may be a point when you need to eliminate certain foods that you notice constantly give you negative responses; you may want to add more of certain foods that give you positive responses. Mindful eating is key to a healthy, whole body-mind connection.

Lead Nutrition Action Step Planning

Hope

I'm sure that many people can agree that believing any false worldview is going to have a negative psychological effect on us. Our worldview is how we relate to others and shapes the way we live. If this is true of the beliefs we place in this world, then the most powerful thing that makes us mentally healthy is hope and vision. In the article "The Proven Path to Mental Health," Jon Bloom states, "The human psyche is designed to operate on hope."[6] We become more mentally healthy the more we are hopeful. Our inner selves are hope machines. Our psyche burns hope like our body burns energy. Just like our physical bodies can't run without energy, so our lives run dry without hope. To keep going, there has to be hope and vision for a future. With hope and vision, there is a drive to change and grow, and possibilities are endless. Without hope and vision there is fear, lack, and shame, and it feels like our energy circuit has been cut. Yet you have to remember that you can't live on vision and hope alone; you have to take action on it.

First, what is hope? According to Merriam-Webster's Dictionary, hope is "a feeling of expectation and desire for a certain thing to happen." "A feeling of trust." If we have to trust something, trust our experiences, trust God. We should ask ourselves, "Can we really trust/put faith in these things?" Take time to meditate on what you can/can't trust. So now I ask, where does your hope come from? Does it come from yourself? Does it come from someone you look up to? Does it come from experience? Does it come from God?

One thing I'm sure many of us have experienced in our lives is that we have failed ourselves and can't seem to always trust ourselves with everything. Others have failed us, and we can't seem to always trust even those we care about most.

Vision

What is vision? It is something you see by creating what the future holds in your mind. Without vision, you will more than likely remain stagnant. This is why your mind is so powerful: You can create your reality with your thoughts. Humans on average have thousands of thoughts per day running through their mind. What if your thoughts were mostly about creating a vision for your life where you pursue your dreams and achieve what you desire? That is something you can hope for! Now, don't get me wrong, I am a firm believer in mindfulness and being present in the moment and enjoying exactly where you are right now. At the same time, you want life to happen for you in the clear vision you desire rather than let it blindly take you wherever the wind blows, only later realizing you never wanted to go in that direction. In short, you have to lead your mind, not let it lead you.

The goal is to guard, strengthen, and renew our mind. We create strongholds in our mind that actually hinder us from seeing things in a new light, creating vision, or hearing God. According to Merriam-Webster's Dictionary, a stronghold is "a place of security or survival." We create strong beliefs that become embedded so deep within us that we tend to use them as security to survive, like a wall is security for a home. These walls need to be broken down in order to renew our mindset into seeing the view behind those walls. This leads to freedom.

The brain is such an interesting part of our body. We tend to think that whatever thoughts jump into our minds must be true. That is a lie in itself. As humans, we tend to lie to ourselves all the time because the brain works in such a way that it sees what it wants to see. Everyone sees a different picture. On some of Dr. Joe Dispenza's videos and podcasts, he talks about the fascinating topic of the optic nerve that connects to our brain and sends more pulses forward to our eyes than our eyes send to our brain. Our brain is telling us what to see.[7] This is why we can't always trust what we see or trust what we think. Check out some of Dr. Joe Dispenza's videos, and you will be incredibly inspired about how powerful your brain is in creating your reality.

There is a verse in the Bible I love so much that when I'm reminded of it, I say, "Ooooooh, ouch, that's good!" Proverbs 15:14: "A wise person is hungry for knowledge while a fool feeds on trash."[8] When trash goes into the trash bin, you've got to empty it, right? Just like in our minds, if there's trash going in, we're going to have to empty the trash. Where do you think that trash goes when it's time for you to empty it? It explodes on your family, friends, coworkers, and other people you interact with. Is it worth it? Not at all. So I ask, what are you feeding your mind?

Just like the food you put into your body fuels you, there is fuel you put into your mind. For your physical body, some food makes you smarter (brain food), some food has empty calories that is neither good or bad (it's just junk food), and some food is toxic (poisonous to your body). To produce great results, you need to be faithful to your body and mind. What are you listening to? What kind of movies are you watching? What kind of music are you listening to? What type of conversations are you involved in? Whatever data your brain is taking in, you begin to reprogram it to believe the things it hears or focuses on. Do you want to feed your body or mind with junk?

Gratitude

A favorite thing of mine is to spend time in states of gratitude. Our minds have the ability to create our current reality. Have you realized that when you focus on a certain material item you begin to notice it everywhere, or if you focus on the positive things in life, it seems that you can find the good in most everything? Those who are constantly stressed in life will create stressful situations wherever they go. It's the same for those who are looking for the negative in others; that's what they will find.

Growing up, my mother and father raised us kids to be grateful for the little things. When we got to go on a camping trip instead of receiving toys, they taught us to be grateful for experiences instead of things in life. When we had a challenge, they taught us to be grateful because we are still alive, and it could always be worse. We learned that challenges build our faith to prepare us to be strong for the next season. In this, I am very grateful for learning at a young age the power of gratitude for it has gotten me through many hard times in life.

In two words, my father describes me as "free spirit." He defines "free spirit" as someone who doesn't get tripped up by the circumstances of life. He says that I've always had a way to see circumstances or challenges as an opportunity for growth or to somehow find joy and beauty in them. I have to say it's from learning about gratitude that's allowed me to see life this way. Thanks, Mom and Dad!

Throughout most of my life, I have kept a gratitude journal or taken the time to meditate on what I am grateful for that day. It could be big or small. Even those days when it felt like I couldn't be grateful for anything, somehow there was at least one thing in life I could find. This has changed my mindset and has rewired my brain to think like this. I know this is also true for many leaders around the world who are making a difference in their own lives and in the lives of others.

Stress

One thing we know about leaders or achievers is that we tend to be driven people who have a goal in mind and want to reach it. We tend to do everything in our power to make something happen and accomplish what we set our minds to. We are generally those who are constantly thinking of others. I don't know about you, but I will personally think of what is best for someone else and make sure they are OK before I even consider what is best for myself. Sounds selfless, right? This may seem like you are doing the right thing, but in the long run, it is an exhausting ride, and over time, you will realize how this takes toll on your health and relationships.

Our subconscious mind is one million times more powerful than our conscious mind. It takes commitment and awareness to live in a way that supports your health on all levels. With the chaos of life, you are asking your glands, organs, liver, gallbladder, kidneys, adrenals, thyroid, brain, and digestive system to cope with the rush you are putting it through. We are not wired to cope with constant pressure, perceived or real, nor are we equipped long term to eat poor-quality food and lead sedentary lifestyles strapped to our computers and cell phones.

There will only ever be 24 hours in a day. How you spend your time is entirely your choice. Your perception of what you need to do is up to you. Today, in women especially, there is the urge to fit as much in as possible. Many years ago, the man was the one who worked for the household, while the woman stayed at home to nurture the children and prepare for the husband. Nowadays, due to changes in social norms, women's rights, the need for women to be equal to men, and the rush of life has caused women to carry an overload more than ever before in history.

In the book Rushing Woman's Syndrome, Dr. Libby Weaver[9] explains that when the woman used to have one job of taking care of her family, she now has three or more jobs including her own career, taking care of family, and maybe some projects on the side. Not that the man of the house doesn't work hard, but the reality of women now taking on more than ever is completely valid.

Taking on too much responsibility has gotten many women to the stressful place of feeling like there are not enough hours in a day or days in a week to accomplish all she needs to get done. All she wants is some rest, peace of mind, and maybe a glass of wine to relax. The things that didn't bother her before will now easily irritate her. She may crave high-fat and high-sugar foods and feel that she needs her coffee or five-hour energy drinks to keep her going. Her body begins to ache, and she feels tension all over and desires a massage. Sleep is either deprived or her quality of sleep is negatively impacted. It seems like it never ends.

This is stress.

Stress is a state of feeling physically, mentally, and emotionally drained. The inside of your body feels anxious, the outside of your body aches, and even your brain hurts. What is it that is keeping you stressed? Do you feel the need to measure up to everyone's standards or are your own standards too high?

Are you the one who says YES to everything?

A lot of times, saying yes is just a matter of wanting to help or serve or not wanting to let others down. It isn't intended to be a bad thing because you really want to help your friends, coworkers, business, and family. But think about it. Are you doing more harm than good when you don't have enough energy to give to yourself? Are you fully able to give to others in the way you really want to?

To not dwell on the stress you are feeling, you need to change your mindset and energy on how to actually get better.

→ Take time out of your daily/busy schedule for yourself.

→ Express your feelings, including worries, fears, anger, sadness.

→ Start doing some volunteering around the community (usually when you do things for others, you begin feeling better about yourself).

→ Start expressing gratitude for the life you live, what you have, and the people in your life.

→ Make loving yourself and loving others a priority.

→ Choose among the opportunities that come your way that offer growth, and learning.

What are your normal go-tos when you tend to stress out? Do you like to veg out on the couch with your favorite box of chocolates or bag of chips? Maybe it is going out for a drink with some friends at the local bar. As appealing as these activities may sound, they do little to reduce the tension that builds up inside a stressed-out body. To effectively release stress, we need to activate our bodies' natural relaxation response and find ways to actively pursue relaxation techniques, such as taking time alone for different types of meditation, deep breathing, yoga, and exercise. Doing so will increase mental alertness, your body will feel capable of more, and you will feel energized all over.

It seems hard to find time to get away from work, family, kids, and doing things you love. There just isn't enough time in one day, is there? If that's how you feel, this is where you need to change your mentality. You would be pleasantly surprised that the more you are able to get away and spend by yourself to focus on balancing your lifestyle, the more you will see the pieces you have never been able to fit before falling together. How do you do this when you feel there is no time? Are you a planner? If not, then this may be the first step to changing your lifestyle to be more intentional.

I've learned that people are more likely to achieve something if they are more intentional with their time. If you have no idea what you are doing the next day and if you don't set intentions or see yourself accomplishing a task, it is more than likely not going to get done. If you don't already have a planner or a phone with a calendar, I suggest you start using one. Look at the week ahead of you and schedule time for yourself as well as the tasks you want to complete.

You may need to make an effort to wake up a half hour earlier than normal, you may need to leave your office during your lunchbreak to go on a brisk walk, or in the evening, you may need to take the time for a bath and/or light some candles and listen to some soothing music before falling asleep. You might want to download a yoga app or a soothing half-hour video or music to help you wind down.

Taking relaxing steps like these will help more than you could ever expect. Something that really helped me before I became a yoga instructor was online yoga videos I followed. I've used a few half-hour videos on the yoga mat, with my lights off and candles lit, to breathe and relax my body and mind. Yoga also lengthens and strengthens my entire core, making me feel stronger mentally and physically.

Lead Mental Action Step

First, rate yourself on a scale of 1–10 where you are at with your mental state. Second, choose one step you can take to get closer to a level 10. What can you do to strengthen your mental capacity or direct your thoughts toward vision and possibility?

_____
_____
_____
_____
_____
_____
_____
_____
_____
_____
_____
_____
_____
_____
_____
_____
_____
_____
_____
_____

Lead Your Emotions

Emotions

As much as our joints, muscles, cells, and other body parts are connected, so are our emotions connected with our mind and body. I don't know if you have noticed, but our society has made it normal to suppress our emotions. It is normal to not deal with them or to know how to respond to people who are showing emotion. There are times we feel guilty or shameful for feeling a certain emotion if we or others see it as a "bad" emotion.

Our emotions are not guides; they are gauges to show us how our heart is doing. Self-awareness is key here because if you only trust your emotions, you will be led astray. Whenever you begin feeling emotions of peace, joy, anger, frustration, love, and so on, you will want to realize where those feelings are coming from. For example, if it is an emotion that causes pain or confusion, you may react negatively to the circumstance based on that emotion. If you feel love, joy, or peace, you may react in a positive way to the circumstance. Whatever emotion you focus on will create a reaction. Remember, all your emotions are important; otherwise, they wouldn't exist. Have you experienced someone who reacted by yelling or saying something negative to you? Maybe you wondered where that came from. Did that make you feel good about yourself or want to listen to them? Most of the time, people will react in a negative way based on something they are insecure about within themselves. This is why it's very important to learn where your emotions are coming from and why you react the way you do.

If you feel frustrated, you have to be aware of why you are frustrated. There is a gauge in your heart telling you you're frustrated. If you feel the emotion of anger, again there is a gauge in your heart that wants you to be aware. Your reactions affect your relationships and those around you, so having awareness of the way you react is important. The emotion you feel is trying to show you how your heart is doing. If you are intentional with your self-awareness, you can still feel any emotion and respond in a healthy way that will not negatively impact others. It takes a lot of inner work to clarify, but it's worth it! You no longer need to let your emotions rule you. An easy way to put it is, "Think before you speak."

People you know and people you don't know experience the same emotions you experience. You're not the first to feel anger, frustration, hate, and so on, and you're not a bad person if you feel these emotions. The only difference is you don't need to be bound by your emotions; you can free yourself from being controlled by them, and you're the only one who gets to choose if you let them control you or if you take control of your emotions. I love the illustration of Jesus in John 11:35 of the Bible: Jesus was moved by compassion and wept.[10] He felt it all. Even if you feel no one understands you, please know that you are never alone.

It's always nice to talk and share with someone who can guide you to places you never thought to look. If you've never seen a counselor or therapist, know that there are certified professionals who can help guide you through blind spots of your past, hurts, and pains that you can't break through alone.

Personally, I had to learn how to feel. I didn't seem to allow myself to feel emotions, especially negative ones. I always thought as long as I was helping everyone else, I would be OK. As I became more self-aware through the help of a counselor and my own practices, I have been able to articulate my feelings. This has allowed me to heal from wounds I never knew I had. I learned it was OK to feel and not to suppress emotions like anger and frustration, yet I didn't have to let those feelings control my life. I also realized places where I was my healthiest or where I was allowing unhealthy habits into my life.

If you have seen a traditional medical doctor but you have not gotten the answers you need, I highly recommend consulting a neorolink practitioner. This system of treatment protocols reconnects the brain to the body when disconnect has occurred as a result of any number of different reasons. I have been seeing a neurolink practitioner, and he has helped me in ways I didn't even know were possible. I also recommend this system to anyone with post-traumatic stress, emotional trauma, viruses, autoimmune diseases, and so on.

The Best Yes

It's absolutely crucial we become aware that our emotional health puts a toll on our physical body, and without proper support, chronic problems can result. Usually those who want to serve and lead well will say yes to most everything because they want to show they are capable, they want to please others, they want to get things done, or they don't want to let anyone down. Believe me, for most of my life, this was me! When we say yes, we are committing a lot more than our word; we are committing our time, heart, soul, emotions, and mind.

In The Best Yes: Making Wise Decisions in the Midst of Endless Demands, author Lysa TerKeurst says, "The decisions you make today matter. Every decision points your life in the direction you are about to travel. No decision is an isolated choice. It's a chain of events. If you choose wisely, your future will reflect that. But if you don't choose wisely, the decisions you make now will take you to places you don't want to be later."[11] I have seen in my own life where I have made decisions because I wanted to make others happy or I didn't want to let them down. In other words, I made my decisions based on other people's needs or desires. These were not the wisest decisions because they led me in a direction I never wanted for myself anyway. You see, even the decisions that seem so small today can affect your future. Setting priorities and boundaries is crucial to your well-being. A solid "no" is not a bad thing; it is a commitment and clarity to yourself and others of where you want to go. When you find yourself wanting to say yes and commit to something, ask yourself, Why am I doing this? Is it pointing me in the direction I really want to go? Will it be filling myself and others up rather than depleting me or them? Ask yourself, Is this my best yes?

Lead Emotional Action Step

First, rate yourself on a scale of 1–10 where you are at with your emotional state. Second, choose one step you can take to get closer to a level 10. Where do you feel you need to create more self-awareness in your emotional state?

Lead Emotional Action Step Planning

What Is Your "Why"?

It's never about what you do that defines you; it is who you are BE-ing in everything you do that defines you. I don't know about you, but I can get caught up in what I am doing and think that it is the most important aspect of my life, as opposed to who I am being that makes me who I am. In this day and age, there is so much comparison between what others are doing and what we are not doing that we can get caught up in feeling like our career is our identity. Today, especially for millennials, there is a pressure to succeed, to hustle, and to be on top. Because of this, our society begins to define what success means. After talking to countless millennials, I have found that they feel as if they are not successful unless they have a career, make an impact, or earn a lot of money. It begins to drive everything they do. Even if it's not money driven, it is somehow success driven by how many hours they work, who they are impacting, and how hard they are hustling. It begins to consume them and seems to define them.

I will never forget a time after I moved back to the Seattle area after living in Los Angeles and then doing mission work traveling the world for a year. I was working at Starbucks as I was transitioning into the next season of life when someone asked me what I was doing back in Seattle and working at Starbucks. They said, "Weren't you living the dream back in LA?" At first, I was a bit irritated by the question. I found myself wanting to defend what I was doing now and that I was still living the dream—it just looked a little different. Before, I was trying to climb some ladder that I thought would reach a place where I would feel fulfilled in my career. What I realized from this experience is, what I do doesn't matter as long as I keep my intention, focus, purpose, and alignment of my "why" in everything I do.

You can have an amazing career and be driven to do well while knowing that it does not make you who you are. Coming to those reality-check moments of why we are doing what we are doing is a game changer in the direction we want to go in our careers. If we are working too hard to rise up the corporate ladder or run a nonprofit or start our own business, we need to know what matters to us because our career is where we spend a lot of our time and energy. We must remember not to let it become who we are, but it had better be worth putting pieces of ourselves into it.

This is where choosing core values comes in. One of my mentors taught me about these values for my personal and professional life. Going back to your values when you come up against trials, questions, or next steps will help you decide what the wisest things to do are. Your values become your foundation for why you do what you do. I'll leave you with a quote from one of my favorite books by Simon Sinek, Start with Why, "People don't buy what you do they buy why you do it."[12]

Lead Values Action Step:

Go through the list of values to follow and choose up to 6 values that resonate with you. Do this for both your personal and professional life. Then define each value with a sentence or two. You may add values if they are not listed here.

When you become clear on what you value, you will be able to take on opportunities rather than distractions. This will bring clarity for any decision-making in your personal and professional life.

Achievement/Drive	Empathy	Justice
Adaptability	Endurance	Kindness
Adding Value	Energy	Knowledge
Adventure	Enthusiasm	Leadership
Aesthetic	Environment	Learning
Affection (Love/Caring)	Equality	Location
Aliveness	Excellence	Love
Arts	Fairness	Loyalty
Authenticity	Fame	Nature
Awareness	Family	Partnership
Beauty	Fast Paced	Passion
Bliss	Financial Gain	Patience
Caring	Flexibility	Perseverance
Certainty	Focus	Pleasure
Challenging Problems	Forgiveness	Respect
Change & Variety	Friendship	Reliability
Charity	Fun	Reputation
Chivalry	Giving	Security
Clarity	Gratitude	Self-Respect
Coaching	Growth	Simplicity
Commitment	God	Spontaneity
Communication	Happiness	Strength
Community	Health	Synergy
Confidence	Honesty	Travel
Discovery	Humility	Vulnerability
Effectiveness	Impacting	Willingness
Economic Security	Intimacy	Wholeness
Ethical Practice	Joy	Wisdom

Lead Career Action Step Planning

_____
_____
_____
_____
_____
_____
_____
_____
_____
_____
_____
_____
_____
_____
_____
_____
_____
_____
_____
_____
_____
_____
_____
_____
_____
_____
_____

Finances are a Tool

Finances are always a funny topic for me because I never really cared about money until I realized it was a tool that could be used to positively affect more lives. I used to see money as a way to have more stuff for the sake of having stuff. I never worried if I would have enough money because life always seemed to work out financially for me.

Have you ever had a dream you wanted to pursue, yet finances got in the way? How about a friend or someone in need you wished you could have given a meal, a gift, or money to support them, but you just didn't have enough to meet your own needs? I have been in both places and realized how much it has stopped me from doing the big things in life I desire but could have done with proper resources.

There are so many people right now, maybe even you, who are in large amounts of financial debt. The weight you carry around haunts you. The more you spend, the worse you feel because you are burdened with the fact that you owe money. We all have our own definitions of what it means to be "financially free."

Money is a tool. It can be a tool for personal gain, or it can be used intentionally and purposefully for the needs around you. I want you to ponder on your own life and think, If I didn't owe anyone any more money, how would I feel? And if I could use money as a resource, what would I do with it?

There are a few ways to see your money as a tool. A lot of us never grew up knowing what to do with our money besides spending it on the things we wanted. For our money to go to the places we desire, we need to steward it well. If you are a steward of your finances, that means you have stewardship, which is defined by Merriam-Webster's Dictionary as "the conducting, supervising, or managing of something." This means to take care of your money well. There is wisdom in spending and saving your money for a purpose and being intentional with every dollar.

If you never learned how to save your money, where you should invest, or what to do with your money, this may be a good time for you to find a financial advisor or mentor who has been successful in stewarding their finances and learn from them. You can do far more than you could ever imagine with properly managed finances. What if money got into the hands of all the right people who wanted to be generous with it? Imagine what could be possible for you, your family, your community, and the world.

Lead Financially Action Step:

First, rate yourself on a scale of 1–10 where you feel financially satisfied. Second, choose one step you can take to get closer to a level 10 Remember, there are so many ways you can be generous if you had the financial means to do so! What does that look like for you?

Lead Financially Action Step Planning

Living Life With Others

I don't know about you, but I realized I cannot do life alone. Every time I have tried, it has left me feeling lonely and like something is missing. In the English Oxford Living Dictionaries, I found a description that explains community well. It is "the condition of sharing or having certain attitudes and interests in common."

When you engage in all of your interests and goals alone, it not only leaves you feeling lonely, but it is also harder to fully enjoy life and accomplish the things you desire. There is something about people coming together to share common ground, to encourage one another, and to talk with one another through life's greatest joys, fears, and challenges.

Personally, the seasons where I have been the most fearful, where life has been the most challenging and scary, is when I have needed community the most. Who I am today is not because I have done it on my own; it's because others have helped shape, mold, and guide me. Have you ever felt like you were alone in something? Maybe you feel that your story isn't as important as others? Maybe you feel that people won't relate to you. Yes, me too. There are other people who have been where you are now, who have walked where you want to go, and who are willing to be right beside you during the seasons of life you encounter. There will be people to uplift, motivate, and challenge you to be your best.

Remember, who you spend your time with is who you become. The five people you spend your time with most is who you become like. Think about it. Is your community uplifting or draining you? Are you finding yourself growing as an individual and in other areas of your life? Do you feel free to be yourself?

Lead Community Action Step:

First, rate yourself on a scale of 1–10 where you feel satisfied with your community. Second, choose one step you can take to get closer to a level 10. Think about what a supportive, loving community looks like to you.

_____
_____
_____
_____
_____
_____
_____
_____
_____
_____
_____
_____
_____
_____
_____
_____
_____
_____
_____
_____

Work Hard, Play Hard

I love to have fun. I also love to get things done. When I'm in focus mode wanting to finish a project or a task, I love to get it done first and then not think about any work later. Some people, on the other hand, love to have fun first and think about work later. When you work hard, both of these ways can work as long as you make sure to enjoy yourself along the way. I like to say, "Work hard, play hard."

I've noticed in our society today that we take pride in how hard we work. Many people prioritize work over fun any day, especially if they like their work. There are many families who suffer because the parents work so hard that they neglect the crucial need to have fun with their family and friends.

From my experience, if you do not have fun and enjoy the process of getting where you want to go, you will eventually burn out, run dry, and not be fulfilled. Some people believe the harder you work, the better life is, and the faster you will get to your destination. Yes, working hard is a good thing, yet if you work hard without enjoying the process, then is it really worth it? That means you may have to schedule fun into your calendar. I personally love the work I do so I can easily work all day. Knowing myself, I need to intentionally prioritize fun activities in my life that give my brain a rest from thinking too much.

Dream

I want to remind you to give yourself permission to dream! You may be a huge dreamer but don't put anything into action. On the other hand, you may try to just get by every day and forget what you actually care about and that it's OK to dream. When we have nothing to look forward to except the day before us, we can feel like we don't have much to live for. Even if you are in a season of staying grounded right where you are, list the things you desire most in life. You can call this a dream list or a bucket list, or you might even choose to create a vision board.

One thing I have on my dream list is to visit every country in the world. Seems extreme? It is what I personally desire and feel is important for my forward propulsion. I plan my life keeping this goal in mind. It keeps me looking toward a specific target and gets me excited to see something on the horizon that brings me the most joy. It's more than OK if your dream is different from mine. Don't worry about what anyone thinks of your dreams, and don't judge others for theirs.

You may be young and excited to dream up your future, you may feel like you don't have any dreams or know where to start, or you may be headed toward retirement and dream only about the day when you retire. It doesn't matter where you are in your journey; it is OK to dream big dreams. There should be no limits to those dreams. Also, remember, the point of dreaming is not to think that something is so far off that it's hard for you to want to do anything to work toward it. Your dreams should inspire you to take small steps toward them daily. It is possible!

Have you created a bucket list or dream list? Have you created a vision board? If not, I challenge you to do so. You can always add more at any point in your life. Reading your list or seeing your board will encourage you to pursue what fulfills you and what you look forward to through all seasons. Then you need to visualize yourself there. Whatever that dream is, practice daily actually imagining that dream being a reality. If you see yourself there and make it feel so real by the way you feel, smell, and taste that dream, it becomes more real and tangible to you.

Recall when you were having the time of your life, a time when you had such joy that you didn't want it to end. Meditate on that and then DO more of that. If you say you don't have enough time, I challenge you to consider that you don't have enough time to miss out on these moments! From my own knowledge, no matter what you believe (even if you believe in reincarnation), you only have this one life exactly the way you are. What is going to matter to you in the end?

Lead Fun Action Step:

First, rate yourself on a scale of 1–10 where you feel satisfied with your fun. Second, choose one step you can take to get closer to a level 10. What does a life of fun and fulfillment look like to you?

Lead Fun Action Step Planning

Lead Your Contribution

I love this quote by Albert Schweitzer: "The only really happy people are those who have learned how to serve." Have you ever had that feeling of fulfillment after you contributed to someone's life, bought someone in need a lunch just because, supported an organization, or given to a hungry kid in Africa or a street kid in your city? That is because we, as humans, are designed to serve.

Stephen G. Post, Ph.D., professor of preventive medicine at Stony Brook University in New York and author of The Hidden Gifts of Helping states, "When people just think about giving, the body doles out feel-good chemicals such as dopamine, which has a soothing effect, and possibly serotonin, one of the brain chemicals we treat depression with. They feel joy and delight—helper's high." [13]

We live in a massive world with billions of people who roam it. Everywhere you go, you can see a need. Nonprofits, projects, and businesses are constantly being created to serve others because there will always be a need in this world. You are someone who has talents, skills, and abilities that can transform lives, whether you think so or not. It might be in your family, your workplace, place of worship, across the globe, or in your own backyard.

Before you go out helping anyone and everyone to receive the benefits of this "helper's high," you have to realize that it only works if you actually care about those you are helping. If you do not, then eventually this obligation can turn into resentment and will likely create emotional and psychological stress. Never give out of obligation; only do it if you want to and genuinely care!

I want to remind you that you are on this planet, right now, just the way you are to serve, on purpose. You may not feel it or know what to do right now, but when you take your passions and align them with your skills, talents, and abilities, you will find the sweet spot that sets your soul on fire.

Servant Leadership

I want to remind you that you are on this planet, right now, just the way you are to serve, on purpose. You may not feel it or know what to do right now, but when you take your passions and align them with your skills, talents, and abilities, you will find the sweet spot that sets your soul on fire.

Robert K. Greenleaf, founder of non-profit Greenleaf Center, published a landmark essay called, "The Servant as Leader," launched the modern-day servant leadership movement, which is now a principle that many sought-out global leaders teach. Greenleaf said, "The servant-leader is a servant first. It begins with the natural feeling that one wants to serve, to serve first."[14]

Let others see you serve and encourage others to serve, too. Make sure your team, family, or whomever you lead knows you care about them. It's not about how much you know; it's about how much you care. Invest in your people. They want to spend time with you. Know that time with them is valuable. Be willing to serve anywhere and do anything. Remember, you aren't too good to clean toilets. If you remember why you do what you do, it doesn't matter what you are doing.

Lead Contribution Action Step:

First, rate yourself on a scale of 1–10 where you feel satisfied with your contribution. Second, choose one step you can take to get closer to a level 10. What is one area in your life that you can see yourself contributing to?

Creating Sustainability Connected All Together

As I mentioned earlier in this book, there will only ever be 24 hours in a day. How you spend your time is entirely your choice. Your perception of what you need to do is up to you. It's easy to say, "Oh, I will do that later" or "Tomorrow I will change." Get clear on the things you desire and then prioritize them. As you learned in this book, all these elements make up your whole life. You are a whole person and every element of your life matters in order for you to live to your fullest potential. You may not love lists or your calendar, but they will be your best friend in making sure you get where you want to go and who you want to be. No one else can do it for you; it's up to you to lead your whole life. Remember, you serve the world best when it's coming from the outpour of your overflow. The world is waiting for you to be fully yourself, the whole you!

LEAD YOUR *Whole*

Where are you on a scale of 1-10?

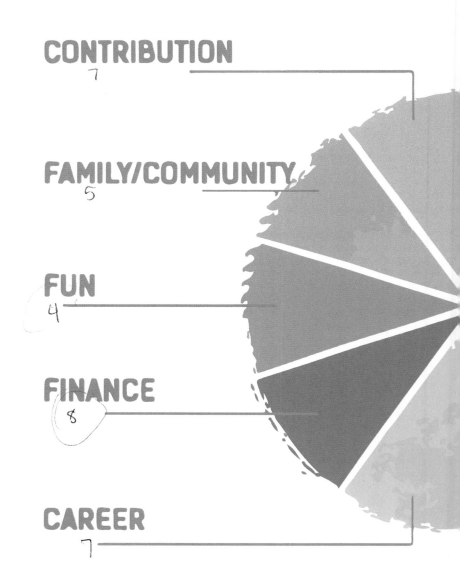

CONTRIBUTION
7

FAMILY/COMMUNITY
5

FUN
4

FINANCE
8

CAREER
7

LIFE CIRCLE

BODY MOVEMENT
6

NUTRITION
6

MENTALITY
4

EMOTIONS
4

SPIRITUALITY
7

Notes

[1] Andy Stanley. *Visioneering*. Colorado Springs, Colorado: Multnomah Books, 1999. Print.

[2] Jessica Dahl and Christina Barnes. The Wholeness Journey Journal. February 1, 2018. Print.

[3] Richard Brennan. *Change Your Posture, Change Your Life*. Wells Street, London: Watkins Publishing. 2011. Print.

[4] Carl Jung. "Ordinary People Act From Fear and Guilt. Extraordinary People Act on Their True Desires." www.theascent.pub, October 10, 2018, accessed October 12, 2018. https://theascent.pub/ordinary-people-act-from-fear-and-guilt-extraordinary-people-act-on-their-true-desires-3a68f3ab12bd

[5] Dominique Gummelt, PhD. "Proof that the Human Body was Made to Move." *www.acefitness.org,* February 4, 2015, accessed January 5, 2019. https://www.acefitness.org/education-and-resources/professional/expert-articles/5282/proof-that-the-human-body-was-made-to-move

[6] Jon Bloom. "The Proven Path to Mental Heath." *www.desiringgod.org*, October 30, 2017, accessed Sept 20, 2018 https://www.desiringgod.org/articles/the-proven-path-to-mental-health

[7] Dr. Joe Dispenza. June 26, 2018. YouTube. "The Mind-Body Connection." YouTube.com, June 26, 2018, Accessed October 15, 2018. *https://www.youtube.com/watch?v=1NhnVlfE4Go*

[8] *Chronological Life Application Study Bible*. Proverbs 15:14 NLT. Tyndale House Publishers Inc., 2012.

[9] Libby Weaver. *Rushing Woman's Syndrome*. London, United Kingdom: Hay House Ltd. 2017. Print.

[10] *Chronological Life Application Study Bible*. John 13:11 NLT. Tyndale House Publishers Inc. 2012.

[11] Lysa TerKeurst. *The Best Yes*. Nashville, Tennessee: Nelson Books, 2014. Print.

[12] Simon Sinek. *Start with Why*. London, England: Penguin Group Inc, 2009. Print.

[13] Stephen G. Post, PhD. *The Hidden Gifts of Helping*. Audible, Inc. 1997–2018. Audio Book.

[14] Cheryl Williamson. "Servant Leadership: How to Put Your People Before Yourself," *Forbes*, July 19, 2017, accessed October 19, 2018. *https://www.forbes.com/sites/forbescoachescouncil/2017/07/19/servant-leadership-how-to-put-your-people-before-yourself/#1f472d6066bc*

About the Author | Jessica Dahl

Jessica Dahl is a certified yoga instructor, certified wellness and life coach, hair stylist, and entrepreneur. Known to her friends and clients as Jess, she has a unique way of making people feel like anything is possible. At a young age, she started writing down her dreams, which focused on helping people live out their passion with purpose. She says that this is what lights her up the most. In her pursuit, she has led beach fitness boot camps in Southern California, and in 2012, she went on a yearlong mission trip where she lived in eleven different countries and did all types of service work, teaching the teams travel-friendly health and fitness, and worked to fight the injustice of human trafficking. She has co-created non-profits, leadership retreats and global yoga mission trips, as well. Combining all her experiences and her heart for people, Jess is committed to helping people know their worth and value while living their purpose in a healthy and whole way and how to lead others well. When she's not changing the world, you can find her hiking, traveling (probably chasing the sun), dancing, exercising, and trying something new with her friends and family. Random fact: Jess is half Spanish and half Norwegian and has an Asian middle name, Mi Yeon, and when she was eleven years old, she sang with Celine Dion on stage at her concert at the Key Arena in Seattle. Jess says, "I am committed to helping people know their value while living into their purpose in a healthy, whole way." Jess would love to hear from you! Visit her website at *www.yourwholepurpose.com* for coaching, retreats, mission trip experiences, collaborations, or opportunities.

For more information visit
www.yourwholepurpose.com

1. Make the ordinary not so ordinary
2. creating a morning & night routine
   - blue light (b)
   - journal
3. Get outside, move your body
4. Journal
5. Mind engaging activities
6. Self care appt -
7. Travel
8. What to do less or more of (BUJO)
9. The Best yes
10. Try something new - 1x/week.
1. Where do you need to take a break to renew?
2. Appreciation & Gratitude
3. Sleep Smarter (Sean Stevenson) - The Model Health
   Shawn   show

Made in the USA
San Bernardino, CA
08 January 2020